Goo... it's a blessing. Lisa

Was It Irony…Or Was It God?

By Lisa J. Taylor

Dedication

This book is simply about God's perfect timing and never-ending grace and is dedicated to my sister, Terry Salyers, my dad, Ross Taylor, my best friend, Trish McGarvey—as well as the many doctors at West Virginia University and Grant Hospitals who worked miracles in saving my life. I would also like to thank the rest of my family and my friends for constantly keeping me lifted up during some pretty dark days.

Table of Contents

Introduction

I have always had great faith that God was working behind the scenes of my life. Looking back, I can only attribute my life direction and personal decisions to my Lord and Savior, Jesus Christ. Although, it may not have been obvious to me at the many stages of my upbringing or career, God was carefully planning and sculpting my very future. That fact never became more evident to me than on Friday, July 13, 2007—the day of my motorcycle crash—the day my life changed forever.

For a number of reasons, I can't help but to think that in some ways, I am not that different from Job—even though I couldn't be farther from righteousness.

I'm simply a forgiven sinner that continues to be "under construction." Both God-fearing and faithful, Job was unknowingly tested by Satan and God in a series of life-altering events. Satan believed that if Job were stripped of his many blessings, he would eventually curse God. God knew better. As a result of these trials and tribulations, Job eventually lost his family, fame, fortune, and his health. As it turned out, after many seemingly unbearable hardships, and a very difficult (and one-sided) conversation with God, Job eventually realized that God wasn't trying to *ruin* him—He was trying to *refine* him.

God had blessed me beyond my wildest dreams. He had provided the opportunity to work with the Ohio State Highway Patrol—a career I truly loved. He further paved the way for several history-making promotions and the ability to earn three college degrees.

At the time of the crash, I was earning an excellent income and was living in a home that I loved. Things were going well for the girl who prior to working with the Patrol, was earning minimum wage—and until the age of sixteen, lived in a five-room home that didn't even have indoor plumbing.

As you will see, there was significant divine intervention over the course of many years leading up to my horrific motorcycle crash. God methodically and strategically aligned everything in my life—*everything* from my family, to my friends, to my finances. He used both the good experiences, as well as the bad to mold me into who I am today. Most people have no idea that when I was five years old, my babysitter's husband molested me. I share this with you only because I believe that God used even this horrible event to shape my destiny. Not only did I survive that *and* the motorcycle crash, God allowed me to thrive by providing me opportunities to meet and work with people I would not have had otherwise. He stretched me by forcing me to get out of my familiar comfort zones. But most of all, God never left me during two of the darkest times of my life. Some may say that my life has been simply a series of ironies. I now know that irony had nothing to do with it—it was God.

At first blush, who would have believed that our crash would have occurred on Friday the 13th? For people who are superstitious, this is considered a day set aside for evil. I believe that Friday the 13th was simply just another day that God demonstrated His awesome power. Furthermore, while I always expected to be hit by an impaired driver while working the road during my many years as a state trooper—I never dreamed that I would be hit by one while off duty, while on my motorcycle, at around two o'clock in the afternoon!

Early in life, I had always wanted to be a writer. In fact, my goal was to go to college and become a journalist. But, as it always does, life got in the way. I never had the time to sit down and put my thoughts on paper. Without this crash creating the topic and opportunity, I would not have written this book. This endeavor started out as simple court preparation, but slowly evolved into a spiritual journey that resulted in this project.

Chapter 1

The Foundation Begins

**My first grade picture—I'm in the second row,
first from the left**

I remember the day well. It was a clear and sunny afternoon in 1968, I believe, and I was spending part of it with my babysitter. See, in those days, many kids in kindergarten only spent half of their day in school. Since my parents both worked, I had to spend the other half of the day with the baby-sitter—one of my mom's friends. I fondly remember our time together—we would often color in coloring books or watch television. For some reason, on this particular day, my babysitter's husband was home. This generally, was not the case.

I remember sitting in front of their coffee table in their living room, coloring. I was also watching The Uncle Al Show—a kid's show based out of Cincinnati. For some reason, my babysitter went into another part of the house, and left me with her husband. He told me that they had quite a few toys in the back room and motioned for me to follow. I did. When we reached the back room, he proceeded to close the door and began to touch me inappropriately. Although I was only five, I knew that what was happening was terribly wrong. I struggled as much as a five year old could and eventually escaped back into the living room, where I sat for the remainder of my time there. I suspect the babysitter had no idea what had transpired—but I'll never really be sure.

When my dad arrived to pick me up, he was driving his older-model white Cadillac convertible. Because it was such a nice day, he had the top down. When I got into the car, he sensed that I was troubled and asked what was wrong. I remember telling him that I couldn't say. He asked why. I told him that something bad had happened and that since the windows were down, I was afraid that someone would hear me. Forget the fact that the top was down—in my five year old mind, the only thing that mattered was that the windows were down. My dad proceeded to roll the windows up so I could tell him what was on my mind. Once the windows were up, I told him what had happened with the babysitter's husband. Although my dad remained quiet, I could tell that he was furious. His face became red and his knuckles were white as he gripped the steering wheel.

My parents had divorced the year before, so he took me home to my mom and went in to talk with her. He told me to leave the room so he and mom could talk. Although they were whispering, I could hear my dad telling my mom what happened. I remember my dad saying, "I'm going to kill him." That, however, was the last time my parents and I ever discussed the ordeal. In those days, I suspect, very few incidents such as this were ever reported. Perhaps it was the fear of public attention or the fear of putting me through the embarrassment of a trial. Nevertheless, I never heard another word about what happened. In fact, my mom refused to even talk about it. That, I guess, was her way of coping. I, on the other hand, don't mind talking about it. I think this was just another way that my life was shaped. I often wonder if that incident had anything to do with me later becoming a law enforcement officer—someone in pursuit of justice. Was that in my subconscious mind during those critical career decisions? I can only surmise that it was. God took something really, really awful and made from it something positive.

Ironically, even though I remember almost every detail of that day—their home, décor, furniture, what

I was coloring, and what I was watching on televi-

sion—I cannot remember my molester's face.

Chapter 2

On Top of the World

"So the Lord was with him and he prospered everything he did." (2 Kings 18:7)

I mmediately following high school, in 1982, I wanted to go to college to study journalism. Unfortunately, my financial situation was less than desirable. I was working for minimum wage as a clerk at a home center in Middletown, Ohio, trying to save for an education. While I am now certain that given my financial situation, I could have attended college without burdening my parents, at the time, I didn't know enough about the available educational grants or loans to pursue them.

My parents had divorced when I was four, so my brothers, Tom and Allen, my sister Terry, and I lived primarily with our mother, Gerry—who was a waitress at the local Frisch's restaurant. Our father, Ross, with whom we spent our weekends, was a steelworker at AK Steel. Even though I'm sure it was sometimes difficult, my parents always remained good friends. In fact, on major holidays, we were almost always still together as a family. While we always had the necessities, we didn't have a lot extra money. But the two things our parents did make sure we had plenty of were love and an appreciation for hard work. I can still vividly remember mom working late so I would be able to have a homecoming or prom dress—

or whatever the "need of the day" was. I can also remember my dad coming home from the steel mill with pockmarked arms from where the steel burned through his asbestos gloves during his workday. But neither of my parents complained — ever. In fact, even though during high school, my siblings and I wanted to get part-time jobs to help out, our parents forbid us working during the school year. They insisted that we focus on schoolwork — rather than money. My mom always told us that, "once you start working...you never stop."

One day while I was working as a cashier at the home center, I met my first state trooper. At that point, the only things I knew about troopers was that they wore big hats and drove white cars. I didn't know it at the time, but this was one of the biggest turning points in my life—one of the many "God" moments I have experienced. The trooper wasn't in uniform or on duty, but he was wearing an Ohio State Highway Patrol sweatshirt. Aside from the OSP attire, I could have guessed he was either a police officer or in the military due to his "high and tight" haircut and his obvious excellent physical condition. During our short conversation, he encouraged me to apply for the Patrol. He said that the organization had just recently started accepting women as trainees. This trooper went on to say what a great job he had and that he would recommend it to others. I filed that conversation away in my mind.

When I went home that evening, I mentioned to my mom what the trooper had said. She too, encouraged me to at least look into the possibility. So, I

called the Hamilton post and spoke with a sergeant.
I told him that I was interested in talking with him
about a potential career with the Ohio State Highway
Patrol. He and I agreed on a meeting date and time
and we ended our conversation. When the day of
the meeting came, I decided against going. I'm now
ashamed to say that I didn't even call to cancel—I
just didn't show up. When I didn't arrive at the post
for our meeting, the sergeant called me and asked
why I didn't attend our prescheduled meeting. I
apologized and told him that I really didn't think I
wanted to be a state trooper. I further stated that I
just wanted to go to college and would pursue ways
to make that happen. I thanked him for his call and
wanted to simply hang up. Fortunately, for me, the
sergeant didn't give up. He continued to encourage

me to come in and at least talk with him about the Patrol. Begrudgingly, I did just that. When I arrived at the post, the sergeant had me fill out an application. He weighed and measured me as well, to ensure that I met the Patrol's rigid height and weight requirements. After talking with me, he scheduled me to take a test at the OSP Academy to see if I was a suitable candidate to be a state trooper.

On the day that I was scheduled to drive to Columbus, Ohio to take the test, my mom took the day off to go with me. I had never driven anywhere but in and around my hometown—so going to Columbus was a big trip! When I got up that morning, I told my mom that I had changed my mind and that I wouldn't be going to take the test after all. I quickly realized that was a mistake! Mom relentlessly shamed me by saying, "what do you have to lose?" She convinced me that this might just be the opportunity that I had been searching for. Again—begrudgingly—I went.

Mom and I drove from Middletown to the big city of Columbus in my 1972 Ford Pinto. The driver's door was sprung, so I had to get in on the passenger side and crawl over the stick shift to get into the drivers seat. Fortunately, I could get out the drivers door, but I had to lift it up and slam it shut in one swift motion to get the door to latch. During the entire trip, I complained to mom that I didn't really want to be a state trooper—I wanted to be a writer. She continued to encourage me to give the Patrol a try. She wanted to make sure I had no regrets.

Upon our arrival at the Patrol Academy, I discovered that there were about thirty men and women there to take the written exam. Surely, I thought, this effort in futility will end here. We were herded into a large room where the test was distributed. While I don't remember much about the test, I do remember thinking that it contained some extremely odd questions. After the testing, we were sent to the lobby until the tests could be graded. A short time later, an OSP officer came into the lobby and read the names of the people who did not pass the exam. Amazingly enough, I was one of three people who passed! Again—another "God moment." After finding out I had passed the exam, I was told that I could leave, but that someone from the Patrol would be calling me soon.

Several months went by, during which time, I had heard nothing from the Patrol. I assumed that they had forgotten about me. Secretly, I wasn't upset about that fact—because I didn't really want to be a state trooper. I continued to look for ways to go to school. To my surprise however, in early 1983, I received a phone call from the Patrol's human resource section. A lieutenant told me that the OSP had a job for me as a cadet dispatcher in West Jefferson, Ohio. I told him that I didn't even know where West Jefferson was, nor did I know what a cadet dispatcher was or did. He described West Jefferson's location (which was about eighty miles from my hometown) as well as what the job entailed. Basically, I would serve as a dispatcher until I turned 21—at which time; I would agree to enter the Patrol Academy to train to be a state trooper. To say I was apprehensive was an understatement!

When I went home that evening, I told my parents about the call from the Patrol. They were both thrilled. I was less than ecstatic, to say the least. I was only eighteen years old and had never been away from home. The thought of moving to a new city, learning a new job, with no family or friends didn't sound quite so appealing to me. To add insult to injury, I had to cut my hair very short to comply with the Patrol's hair standards policy. It was a good thing that they didn't tell me about having to cut my hair until I agreed to take the job. My hair was so long at that time that it reached the middle of my back. I cried the day I had to cut it. All the while, my mom said, "if you don't like the job—you can move back home—and your hair will grow back."

Before my actual move, I had to find an apartment in the town that would become known as, "West Jeff." My mom, my sister, and I traveled to West Jeff in search of something I could afford. My savings was small and I would only make about $6 an hour as a cadet, so I had to find something really inexpensive. After a long and arduous search, we quickly realized that the only place I could afford in town was in a mobile home park. The trailer park housed a community of elderly folks who really didn't take kindly to a single, young woman moving in—until they found out I was going to work for the Patrol. Then, for some reason, I immediately became an acceptable neighbor. My rent would be $145 a month.

The apartment was extremely small, but clean. Unfortunately, the water had an awful color and sulphuric odor—which made it impossible to drink. It actually stained my shower stall bright orange. My sister, however, made the transition as pleasant as possible. She helped me decorate it and make it as "homey" as it could be. The trailer/apartment that I moved into was unique. In fact, I hadn't ever seen one like it before, nor have I since. It was a trailer factory-made to be two apartments. I moved into the front half, and an older truck driver named Clyde lived in the back half. What was even more humorous is that Clyde and I drove identical cars—the same *year, make, model, and color*! Clyde and I was quite an odd pair—but we got along great. We even cooked out occasionally on our shared patio. Our neighbors must have thought we were a sight!

I remember my first summer living in that trailer. I was working midnights, so I had to sleep during the day. Unfortunately, the trailer became like an oven during the hot summer days. I had no air conditioning, so the temperature inside the trailer would easily rise to over 100 degrees. After being unable to sleep, I took a sheet and a pillow outside and put them under a shade tree. In my desperation for sleep, I resorted to sleeping outside. Surely, it would be more comfortable than the trailer! I desperately wanted and needed to get a good night of sleep, but couldn't afford even one night in a hotel. My neighbors—the Browns—apparently saw me trying to sleep outside. Mr. Brown came over and asked what in the world was I doing. I told him that it was simply too hot to sleep in my trailer. He kindly brought over a small window air conditioner and installed it in my bedroom window. He allowed me to borrow it until I left to enter the academy.

The elderly couple that managed the trailer park also quickly took me under their wings. Mac and Vera McCormick treated me as though I was one of their own daughters. I enjoyed many home cooked meals and fresh vegetables from their garden. Ironically, years earlier, Mac had served as a motorcycle instructor for the Patrol, teaching young recruits how to ride motorcycles. I loved to hear his stories about the "old patrol" and its early motorcycling days! I didn't realize it then, but God was continuing to protect and provide for me during one of the most uncertain times of my life.

So, I officially joined the Ohio State Highway Patrol on February 14, 1983 as a cadet dispatcher. On my first day with the division, I was scheduled to meet my district commander, Captain Thomas Rice (who would later become the Patrol's superintendent). I got up, got dressed, and prepared to drive from West Jeff to Columbus for our meeting. Because our meeting was scheduled early in the day, when I left the trailer park, it was still quite dark. To complicate things, it was extremely foggy too. The fog was so thick that I literally could not see the hood ornament on my car. I'm sure that the weather conditions, my unfamiliarity with the area, as well as my being nervous—all contributed to me turning eastbound in the westbound lanes of US40. As I drove eastbound for a considerable distance, several cars blew their horns at me in an attempt to get me on the right side of the highway. When I realized my mistake, I closed my eyes and drove through the median, praying that I wouldn't hit another vehicle—and miraculously—I didn't! No one knew for a long time how close I came to dying on my first day on the job! God continued his work.

My meeting with Captain Rice went well. He described the district as well as his expectations. Little did he or I know that he would eventually promote me to the rank of sergeant. I was a bit dismayed, however, when he told me that my hair was, "not short enough."

Although I knew that the Patrol required me to have a telephone within the first two weeks of my employment, I simply didn't have the money. Because

I had paid my rent and deposit, as well as paying to have all my utilities hooked up, I was out of money. I was too proud to ask my parents for money, so I was hoping that the Patrol would either not check to see whether I had a phone, or that they would give me a reprieve until I received my first paycheck. I was wrong on both counts. About two weeks into my career, Lieutenant Lou Holben, my post commander called me into his office and inquired as to whether I had a telephone yet. I told him no, but didn't elaborate as to why. He didn't ask any questions, but simply took out his wallet out, pulled out a $50 dollar bill, and slid it across his desk. He said, "Get your phone hooked up. If you can pay me back later, that's fine. If you can't, don't worry about it." Back then, $50 was a lot of money—money that I didn't have. I was eternally grateful for the money and for the fact that he didn't try to embarrass me about my financial situation. I often wonder how other post commanders would have handled that situation. I can tell you that I learned a lot about leadership, compassion, and generosity that day from Lieutenant Holben. And, by the way—I did pay him back.

I spent over two years at the West Jeff post, learning the inter-workings of the Patrol and how to effectively dispatch. In addition to using maps, I best learned the area by riding my motorcycle throughout our area of responsibility. Also during my time there, I learned military courtesy and prepared physically for my eventual entry into the OSP Academy. I also continued to learn the value of money. My budget was meager and I subsisted on a steady diet of Ramen noodles and macaroni and cheese. While I still love macaroni and cheese, to this day, I still cannot even think of eating Ramen noodles! Occasionally, I was able to treat myself to a meal at McDonalds.

During my training period, my "coach," Dispatcher Joe Gorman taught me many things. In addition to the dispatching training and the other valuable and technical skills he taught me, he showed me better than anyone how to shine shoes. That skill served me well in the Academy! The other dispatchers and troopers all contributed to my personal and professional development. Each one taught me valuable skills or lessons that I would take with me throughout life.

My next post commander, Lieutenant Rich Rucker—who nicknamed me "Stubbs," (and who eventually became a major and served on the division's senior staff) would periodically take me out onto US40, follow me in a patrol car, and would time my 1.5 mile run. Lt. Rucker would get on the public address system of his car and yell, "Move it Stubbs, move it!" over and over again. The motoring public probably got a huge kick out of my physical training regimen. During my time I spent with Lt. Rucker, he shared his faith in God and—although he probably doesn't even realize it, he really helped guide me in my spiritual journey.

In April 1985, I entered the OSP Academy and endured the rigorous training required to be an Ohio State trooper. The training was extremely militaristic and it compressed about two years of college into six months. Since the Patrol had not started accepting women into the uniformed ranks until 1978, women were still somewhat of an anomaly. In fact, at the time, there were only about twenty female troopers in the entire organization. During my time there, I learned a true appreciation for teamwork, education, physical conditioning, and time management. It was very apparent early in the program that the cadets not willing to give 100% in those areas did not become Ohio State troopers. I often tell people that I wouldn't take a million dollars for the training I received at the OSP Academy. I also jokingly say that I wouldn't go through it again for a million bucks either. In all seriousness though, the OSP Academy was one of the best things I could have ever done. It not only provided me with a viable and honorable trade, but also taught me discipline and team skills—things

I would use throughout my life. To this day, I am convinced that I survived one of the toughest and finest law enforcement academies in the world.

While in the Academy, we were provided an opportunity to list our top three preferred assignments. This "wish list," was to assist the Patrol leadership in our placement upon graduation. Being from the southern part of Ohio, I simply wanted to stay south of Interstate 70, so I asked to go to the West Jefferson, Springfield, or Xenia posts. The Patrol, however, had other plans for me.

In September 1985, upon my graduation from the Academy, I was sent to Bucyrus. Once again, I was being sent to unfamiliar territory to learn a new job with new people. God was stretching me—forcing me out of my comfort zones. I spent seven wonderful years at the Bucyrus Post. During that time, I learned the job of a state trooper, developed friendships, as well as professional relationships that I would not have had the opportunity to do anywhere else. Again, I used my motorcycle as a valuable tool to quickly and enjoyably learn my new area. Because of the many speech details and work with the local schools, I quickly overcame my fear of public speaking. I became entrenched in the community and was enjoying every minute of it.

Several times early in my career, God revealed His great sense of humor—or taught me humility (I'm not sure which). One day, after I had become some-what comfortable in my position, I was working on US23 in Wyandot County, when I saw a brand new BMW headed northbound at an extremely high rate of speed. When I initiated the radar, I got a readout of well in excess of the posted 55 MPH speed limit. I immediately crossed the median and stopped the driver. When I asked him for his driver's license, registration, and proof of insurance, he told me that he didn't have a driver's license, but that he did have a travel visa. He further stated that, "I'm the prince of Belgium." Believing that he was lying and simply trying to get out of a ticket, I said, "yes, and I'm the queen of England, and I need to see your documentation." I quickly discovered, however, that he was, in fact—the prince of Belgium! I attempted to recover from my misstep. He asked me not to tell anyone that I saw him, as he wasn't supposed to be out and about without his entourage. I readily agreed, telling him that, "I won't tell anyone that I saw you, if you don't tell anyone that you saw me!" I lived in fear for months of that potential complaint—one that I would have been chargeable and one that I would have certainly deserved!

On another occasion, as a young trooper, I was again on patrol, when I was dispatched to a school bus vs. farm tractor fatal crash. I responded as quickly as I could, as I was told that the farm tractor was hauling anhydrous ammonia—which could be deadly and would further exasperate the situation. Upon arrival, I saw both vehicles and a multitude of people working in and around the scene. The sheriff's department, local police, fire department, EMT's, as well as other safety-services personnel were working diligently to tend to the injured. There was also a large plume of what appeared to be anhydrous ammonia above the scene. The back doors of the school bus were open, and my sergeant, Jim Bennett was handing bloodied children to other safety personnel. When I jumped from my patrol car, I grabbed my first aid kit and camera and began to assist in any way that I could. At that time, Sergeant Bennett yelled for me to help him remove children from the bus. I immediately dropped my equipment and ran to help. Sergeant Bennett handed me a young boy who appeared to be about eight or nine years old. He was completely covered in blood and seemed lifeless. Sergeant Bennett told me that the boy was deceased and to place him on the ground. My left hand was right next to the boy's carotid artery, so I felt for a pulse—which I quickly found. I said, Sarge, this boy has a pulse! He's not dead! Sergeant Bennett said "he's dead, Lisa!" I reiterated again that I felt a heartbeat. It was at that point that I discovered that this entire event was a MOCK disaster and that apparently everyone knew about but me! Although Sergeant Bennett has been retired for years, when I do see him, he never fails to bring this story up!

Another embarrassing moment came as I was again working the road. I came upon an abandoned, disabled vehicle on US30 just east of Upper Sandusky, Ohio. The car was partially on the road, so I lit a few flares and placed them around the vehicle before going to search for the occupants. I suspected that they had walked to the Sunoco station just down the road. I went to the gas station and located the vehicle's owners. They had contacted a tow truck, so I offered to take them back to their vehicle. The individuals were very appreciative for my assistance. While we were on our way back to their car, my dispatcher told me that she had a report of a car fire just down the road from me. To my horror, one of the flares had apparently rolled against one of the tires of the disabled vehicle and caught it on fire. When we arrived, their vehicle was completely engulfed in flames. It was one of the most humbling experiences to tell them that I was responsible for the loss of their vehicle. Fortunately, they were extremely understanding and gracious. As you can guess, the call to my sergeant was equally as humbling!

My field-training officer, Sergeant Ernie Howard (who later became a Lieutenant Colonel) taught me the "ropes" of the road. He taught me the importance of accepting responsibility and how important it was to maintain your credibility — both on and off duty. He also stressed the importance of having fun doing whatever career you choose. He encouraged me to further my education as well. It was then that I started my pursuit for an associate's degree through Ohio University. Ernie, who remains a very close friend, was instrumental in helping me along throughout every stage in my career.

The Bucyrus post commander, Lieutenant Ralph Ehrhart, was a fair, but no-nonsense kind of leader who told you exactly where you stood. I always appreciated that. When troopers would come to work, they had to pass his office. When they looked in, they could tell by Lt. Ehrhart's facial expression whether to keep on walking, or to attempt to engage him in conversation. It was rumored that Lt. Ehrhart wasn't thrilled with the thought of having women serve in the uniformed ranks of the organization. But, fortunately for me, Trooper Brenda Smith became the first female law enforcement officer in the Bucyrus area about a year before I arrived. Brenda broke the ice with not only the community, but with the other law enforcement agencies—and with Lt. Ehrhart. I would like to think that Brenda and I changed his mindset about female troopers. After my eventual promotion to Lieutenant, Lt. Ehrhart would later send me a card congratulating me. He signed it, "to the second best lieutenant in the state patrol." I still cherish that note, as it spoke volumes about his evolving attitude about female officers.

After becoming comfortable in my job as a trooper, I had the great honor of training four new officers upon their graduation from the Academy. This experience was invaluable as I climbed the ranks as a supervisor, manager, and leader. I'm proud to say that of the four officers, two were later promoted, and three still serve in the organization. It was very gratifying to know that at least in some small way, I contributed to their professional development.

In 1992, I became the seventh female in the history of the Patrol to be promoted to the rank of sergeant and assistant post commander. I spent three years in that capacity at the Norwalk Post. On my first day on the job, my new post commander, Lieutenant Brooks Hartmann, met me at the door and informed me that my job was to "ensure that he had nothing to do." So, I did just that. Fortunately, the Norwalk Post was due for a biennial inspection. Inspections are huge in the OSP. In essence, they are designed to determine the overall operational and personnel "health" of the facility. Furthermore, the inspections also provide senior staff a snapshot of the post leadership. Senior staff can then make educated and informed decisions about potential changes necessary in the management staff. Lt. Hartmann asked me to take a leadership role in the inspection preparation process. This experience proved priceless later in my career. Again, as God expanded my territory and experience, He provided new challenges. After three years, however, I wanted to gain experience at a busier assignment, so I requested a lateral transfer to the Marion Post, where I spent another year.

At Marion, even though it was only for a short time, I was again exposed to whole new area and

host of co-workers. I was also able to garner experience with criminal investigations in the area prisons.
I also had the pleasure of working for Lieutenant Clarke Kiner. Lt. Kiner was one of the best leaders and ambassadors for the Patrol that I have ever known. He taught me the importance of professionalism—in both appearance and demeanor. But, I remember him best because he always cared for and supported his people.

In 1996, I was promoted to lieutenant and post commander and was reassigned to the Norwalk Post. I was honored to be the first female in the history of the Ohio State Highway Patrol to ever be promoted to that rank. Fortunately, because I was returning to Norwalk, I was going to familiar territory. I knew the staff and was excited to work with them again.

It was there that I "cut my teeth" as a new post commander. I sometimes worked sixteen-hour days because I didn't want the Patrol to regret their decision to make me a post commander. In retrospect, the Patrol didn't put pressure on me—it was all self-induced. Failure to me was not an option. I was afraid that if I failed—it would negatively reflect on every other female officer in the organization. That was one of my biggest fears as a female mentor and leader in the Patrol.

Although I loved the Norwalk area, after about a year, I again requested another lateral transfer—this time to the Mount Gilead Post. I felt that I had learned all I could at Norwalk and wanted to transfer to a busier post. Upon the approval of my transfer, my staff and my areas of responsibility virtually doubled. My new boss, Captain Les Reel was another outstanding leader who helped shape my leadership style—and ultimately my destiny. I watched in awe how he interacted with others under his command. I knew early on in our professional relationship that I would like to emulate some of his traits. He would periodically stop by my house for a Pepsi—at any hour of the day—just to see how things were going. During my tenure at Mt. Gilead, I learned more than I could have ever imagined. God continued to groom me for future responsibility.

After serving about a year at Mount Gilead, I was promoted to the rank of staff lieutenant and served as an assistant district commander at the Jackson District Headquarters. Again, history was made. Another female and I were promoted on the same day to positions that historically had been held only by males.

My new boss was Captain Larry Meredith. Captain Meredith was another great mentor that God put in my path. I instantly took a liking to him. Although he didn't know me well yet, he immediately gave me the necessary encouragement and latitude to do my job. He allowed me to be creative in accomplishing my duties. He often told me that "life is short—do whatever makes you happy." I considered it an honor to have worked for a man who *always* put his family and his faith first. In that capacity, I served for approximately a year and a half before having the good fortune of being promoted to captain and district commander, after Captain Meredith retired. While I have enjoyed every assignment with the Patrol, the

Jackson District will always be one of my favorites—and the one I will always call "home." I found that the people, terrain, and mindset of southern Ohio are all pretty conducive to my personality.

I was the first female to hold the rank of Captain. I was ecstatic, as this was the only promotion in which I didn't have to physically move to another geographic location. As captain, I spent four years at that facility. My staff and I oversaw the operational and staffing needs of our district, which included ten counties (Athens, Hocking, Gallia, Meigs, Jackson, Vinton, Lawrence, Ross, Scioto, and Pike) and approximately two hundred and fifteen employees. It was during this period that I started to feel God pulling me. While I had always considered myself a Christian, I hadn't really gotten serious about my faith. One of the huge turning points in my life was joining a small, 30-member congregation church—Church of the King, in Jackson. It was there that I started diligently studying the Bible and learning the principles of tithing under Pastor Butch Deer. It was during this time that I believe God spoke *audibly* to me on two different occasions. He was trying to direct me on a couple of life issues. I won't share with you the contents of those conversations, because they are deeply personal. I am ashamed, however, that I didn't heed His guidance at the time. Some lessons are learned the hard way. It was also during this time that I began pursuing my bachelor's degree in religion at the Circleville Bible College (now known as the Ohio Christian University). This turned out to be one of the best educational and faith-based decisions of my life. It was there that I really started to study and understand the Bible.

In late 2004, I received a phone call from Colonel Paul D. McClellan, Patrol Superintendent, asking me to meet him the following day at the academy after a promotion ceremony. When we met in the Academy VIP area, he asked me to accept the position of major, overseeing the Patrol's Office of Finance and Logistics Services. This would mean overseeing the finance, facilities, fleet, procurement, the tailor shop, as well as the stockroom components of our statewide organization. He further explained that as a senior staff member, I would assist in leading, guiding, and directing the entire organization. I graciously accepted the position. I had always viewed him as an outstanding leader and looked forward to the opportunity to serve him and the organization in a new capacity. I soon moved to the Columbus, Ohio area and bought my first home in Grove City. I was fortunate to find a wonderful church—Grove City Church of the Nazarene—that, ironically has a huge motorcycle ministry. It seemed like a perfect fit for me. Shortly thereafter, I began working on the fifth floor of the Shipley Building, which houses our general headquarters and became the highest-ranking female in the history of the Ohio State Highway Patrol.

During my tenure there, I had the good fortune of working with a large number of wonderful people. My executive officer, Captain David Dicken was extremely helpful in preparing me for my role on senior staff. He introduced me to many of the players in state government. We worked closely with the

Department of Administrative Services, the Office of Budget Management, the Controlling Board, Legislators, as well as the Governor's office. As I was continuing to learn my role, I finished my bachelor's degree and began graduate school at Franklin University. I was supposed to graduate in May 2008, and retire in 2010 to pursue other interests – or at least that was the plan.

In my OSP uniform

"Just as storms in life are a certainty, so is the provision of God for every storm we will ever face. Life can be messy and bad things will happen, because every crisis and every storm is an opportunity to trust God. He calls us to a heavenly perspective when facing challenging times. He calls us to see them as He sees them - opportunities for His power and purpose to be illustrated in human terms."

- Crosswalk.com -

Chapter 3

Life Changes in the Blink of an Eye

"The Lord gave me everything I had, and they were His to take away." (Job 1:21)

Laura, Jules and me in Minnesota – 2006

In July 2007, I was forty-three years old, in the best shape of my life, living in the home of my dreams, and at the height of my career. I had great family, wonderful friends, and was an avid motorcycle enthusiast. My dad is responsible for my love of motorcycles. He taught me to ride a mini-bike from the time I could walk. My dad, my friends, and I had traveled by motorcycle to over a third of the United States and parts of Canada and had logged over a quarter million miles.

For the last six or seven years, several friends and I had planned and gone on a long motorcycle trip. My friend Mary Pfeifer, who is a lieutenant and post commander at the Marietta Post, and I have been friends for almost twenty-five years. She and I, along with Sergeant Laura Pascuzzi, from Des Moines,

Iowa Police Department, and Dr. Jules Burrian, also of Iowa took turns planning our yearly trips. Over time, we have traveled west into Sturgis, the Badlands, Custer National Park, Mount Rushmore, Crazy Horse, Deadwood, and Devils Tower. We've also explored parts of the Midwest– Ohio, Kentucky, Indiana, Illinois, Missouri, Minnesota, and West Virginia. We have also traveled south to Tennessee, Georgia, and North Carolina, as well as to the coastal state of Maryland. We normally took two weeks for our excursions; however, I had to explain that I could only take one week this particular year, due to my college responsibilities. Unfortunately, I could not—and would not miss two weeks of class. So, we decided that Laura, Jules, and Mary would travel to my home in Grove City to meet. Our plans were for them to arrive at my home on Wednesday, July 11, 2007—which they graciously obliged.

On Thursday, July 12, we all awoke, enjoyed a leisurely breakfast, packed our bikes, and outfitted ourselves in protective gear for our big adventure to the Laurel Highlands of Pennsylvania. Although we all had our own bikes, Mary asked if she could ride along with me, as she likes to sightsee more than drive. I agreed. Jules decided that she would also double up with Laura since Mary and I were going to ride on one bike. I was going to ride my 2001 Yamaha Roadstar 1600, and Laura was riding her brand new Harley Davidson Roadglide. I had just had my motorcycle in for service. A manufacturer's recall was done, a safety check performed, as well as new tires, and an oil change was completed in preparation for our trip.

The morning we left was absolutely picturesque. It was warm, sunny, and pleasant. We took back roads through Ohio with plans to stop in Wheeling, West Virginia at the Wheeling Casino for the night. We had a great day—the sun in our faces, and the wind in our hair. The only problem was a small electrical issue Laura had with her Harley Davidson—which was repaired at the Saint Clairsville, Ohio Harley Davidson dealership. When we arrived at the casino, we checked in, had dinner, and gambled for a while.

The next morning—Friday the thirteenth of July—we got up, ate breakfast, loaded the bikes, and gambled again for a short time. We took off from the casino and headed east. As we traveled through

Mary and me at the Crazy Horse monument
– 2006

Wheeling, we decided to drive through Oglebee Park, as Laura and Jules had never been there. So, we showed them around the park via motorcycle before heading east on US40. We had a morning I'll never forget; for that was the last day I walked normally.

"It is not the cards you are dealt but what you do

with them that counts"

-Anonymous-

Chapter 4

Almost Losing a Limb

"Even when walking through the dark valley of death I will not be afraid, for You are close beside me, guarding, guiding all the way." (Psalms 23:4)

As we rode our motorcycles east on US40, at approximately 2:00 P.M., Mary and I were traveling in the lead; Laura and Jules were lagging a bit behind. We were in an area known as Valley Grove, West Virginia. As we entered a long and sweeping "S" curve, I slowed down and looked into rear view mirror, as I had lost sight of our friends. As

I slowed to 35-40 MPH, Mary looked up, and saw a silver Chevrolet Cobalt coming westbound, around a curve, out of control. She made a verbal utterance that immediately caught my attention. As I looked up, I too, saw the vehicle coming towards us. The vehicle initially went off the right side of the road, and appeared to have clipped a telephone pole. Then, in an apparent attempt to bring his car back onto the road, the driver started to broad slide across the highway. The left rear quarter panel of the Chevy slid almost five feet into my lane. Mary and I hit the Chevy behind the driver's door and followed the line of the vehicle back to the bumper. We were both thrown from the motorcycle. I remember sliding down the highway on my back, thankful that I was wearing a Fieldsheer motorcycle body armored jacket and

Vega helmet. I could feel my helmet bouncing off the pavement. At that point, it seemed like everything was in slow motion. I remember sliding for what seemed like an eternity. I eventually slid off the road, face-up, into a deep ditch. When I looked down, my jeans had been partially ripped from my body and my left leg was mangled beyond belief. My left knee was literally shoved up to my chest, while my boot-less foot and calf were contorted in unnatural positions. I saw multiple compound fractures. My left hand was crushed and bleeding—despite wearing Kevlar motorcycle gloves. My motorcycle was lying partially in the road, and partially in the ditch, just west of me. Mary was lying in the middle of the eastbound lane, not moving, and the Chevrolet was completely in my lane, just west of Mary. I screamed for Mary to determine if she was injured, however, she could not hear me, for my motorcycle's throttle was wide open.

Fortunately, Laura and Jules rounded the curve just after the crash occurred. They were spared witnessing the horrific event. I was so thankful they were not involved. Laura immediately parked her motorcycle and rushed to our aid. Also, fortunately, our crash occurred right in front of a trucking company. Employees from the trucking company came running out to see what they could do to help and called 911. A gentleman came over to me and told me everything would be all right. Someone shut off my bike, so I was finally able to communicate with Mary. She told me she was okay, but she did not want to move, as she did not know the extent of her injuries. Mary knew better than to risk moving. Not only is she a state trooper, but also a volunteer firefighter, as well as a trained emergency medical technician.

Final rest of John P. Walenciej's car

For some reason, I did not immediately feel any pain. In fact, I had an unbelievable peace about the situation —*God's peace, which is far more wonderful than the human mind can understand (Philippians 4:7)*. Although the situation was critical, I intuitively felt that everything would be fine. I asked the gentleman from the trucking company if he thought the doctors would have to remove my leg. He said that he did not know.

While I knew my injuries were severe, fortunately, I couldn't see that an artery had been cut in my left leg. With every heartbeat, blood was gushing from my mangled leg. Had I known about the extensive bleeding, I may have panicked and exacerbated the situation. Fortunately, a lady from the trucking company held a compress on the artery to prevent me from bleeding out. I had no idea how close I came to bleeding to death prior to transport.

When the squad arrived, an emergency medical technician (EMT) came to my aid. I asked him if he thought that my leg would need to be amputated. He responded with a hesitant, "maybe." Even though the squad employees cover a large area, they were, interestingly enough, just down the road after finishing a previous run. Again, God continued to take care of me.

As the squad members tended to us, a middle-aged and disheveled looking man walked over to the edge of the road, where he stared at me from above. His face was blank and emotionless, and he appeared to have trouble walking. I asked him if he was a witness, to which he replied, "what?" I repeated my question and he replied, *"Well you hit me!"* At that point, I yelled for Laura to get the man's keys and driver's license, as I did not want him to leave the scene before law enforcement arrived. His car still appeared to be drivable. The fact that I was riding with two other law enforcement officers the day of the crash was no coincidence. Sergeant Laura Pascuzzi, prevented the impaired driver from fleeing the scene.

We later discovered that the man who hit us was John P. Walenciej, of Brilliant, Ohio. He was arrested shortly thereafter for two counts of driving while under the influence with injury. This was his first DUI. We were also told that he admitted in his statement to authorities to taking 80-mg. of Oxycontin and a host of antidepressants prior to driving. When he was taken to the Ohio County Sheriff's Office for processing, according to the law enforcement officials, he continued to appear disoriented and at some

point lost control of his bodily functions.

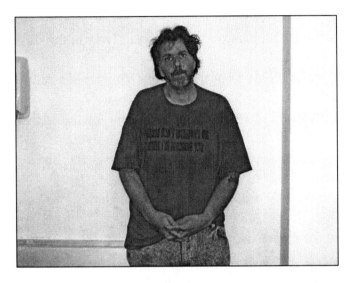

Photo of John Walenciej the day of the crash

The EMT's eventually loaded Mary and me into

separate squads. Laura then came to the door of

the squad and asked me who I wanted her to call.

I initially said, "no one," as I didn't want anyone

seeing me in the condition I was in—particularly my family. Eventually, I realized I would have to do the inevitable. I told her to contact my sister, Terry, but to "soften" the news. I did not want Terry or my dad, to make the six-hour trip to West Virginia in a panic.

Mary and I were both conscious for the trip to Wheeling Hospital. Upon my arrival, the EMT's accidentally dropped one end of the gurney I was on as they were taking me out of the squad. In fact, a large portion of the bone in my left femur fell out onto the pavement. This left me in excruciating pain. Once we entered the emergency room, the doctors attempted to stabilize us and treat our injuries. It was there that the medical staff had to cut my OSP class ring from my left hand. When the doctors tried to straighten my leg, the pain was so severe that I immediately lost consciousness.

Mary was treated and released, but sustained broken toes, broken ribs, ligament damage to her left leg, and a torn hamstring in her right leg. Later, she discovered she also sustained a herniated disc in her neck for which she eventually had to have surgery.

My injuries were significant enough that they decided to airlift me to the closest trauma center in Morgantown, West Virginia. Unfortunately, the weather quickly turned treacherous and I was forced to make the trip by ambulance.

Oddly, on that very day, my good friend, Captain Tina Phillips of the West Virginia State Police was having a family gathering and pool party. Tina and I had met during an assessment center exercise at the Pennsylvania State Police Academy several years earlier. One of Tina's relatives, who lives near the crash scene, came to the party and told her that two female Ohio State Highway Patrol officers on a motorcycle had been involved in a serious crash on National Road. While Tina had no idea that I was traveling through her area, she had the feeling that it had to be Mary and me, and immediately put on her uniform and responded to the hospital — another God thing. I had already been transferred to Morgantown, but Tina actually met Mary at the Wheeling Hospital for the first time. Throughout this ordeal, she proved to be such help in keeping up with the case and showing us great hospitality any time we were in her area, as Mary and I could not attend the first few pretrials due to our injuries.

Final rest of my motorcycle after the crash

Wheeling, WV Newspaper Article

Man Arrested On DUI Charge After Crash

Injures Troopers

Friday, July 13, 2007 – updated: 9:37 am EDT

July 16, 2007

WHEELING, W.Va. — Deputies arrested a man on

DUI charges after a crash injured two off-duty Ohio

State Highway Patrol troopers. Police told NEWS9 that two off-duty troopers were riding a motorcycle early Friday afternoon on National Road in Valley Grove. Deputies said the driver was Lisa Taylor, and the passenger was Mary Pfeifer, who are both highway patrol troopers (from Ohio). A motorcycle collided with a silver car around 2:30 p.m. Police arrested the driver of the car, John P. Walenciej, of Brilliant, right after the accident on driving under the influence with injury charges. As for the victims, crews took Taylor to a Morgantown hospital for what deputies called a bad leg injury. According to the Ohio County Sheriff's deputies, the passenger, Pfeifer, was set to be treated and released from Wheeling Hospital for a broken leg. Troopers are still investigating the cause of the crash.

"Courage is not the absence of fear,

but rather the judgment that something else is

more important than fear"

-Ambrose Redmoon-

Chapter 5

Miracles Performed

"Don't be afraid, for the Lord will go before you and will be with you; He will not fail nor forsake you." (Deuteronomy 31:8)

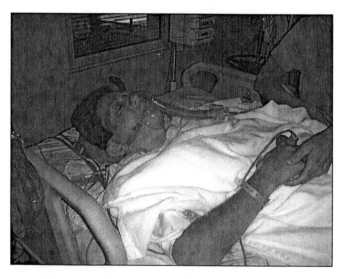

At WV University Hospital – just taken off the ventilator

Upon my arrival at West Virginia University Hospital in Morgantown, I was still unconscious. We crashed near the Ohio-West Virginia border. Fortunately, the West Virginia State Police knew many of the troopers at the adjoining St. Clairsville Post, in Ohio and the communication between the two began early on. News was already starting to spread about our crash and it's severity. You see—law enforcement is a very tight-knit community.

Laura called my sister, Terry to break the news. My good friend, Dianna White, a lieutenant with the OSP called my dad. My sister and my niece, Erin Hubbard then headed to my dads to pick him up for the trip to Morgantown. Fortunately, my friends Dianna White and Trish McGarvey, both fellow motorcyclists, with whom I've ridden with many times, graciously decided to escort my family on the long trip.

When Terry, Dad, Erin, Dianna, and Trish arrived, they discovered the seriousness of my injuries. The doctors informed them that I very well might lose my leg. I was already wearing an external fixator on my upper left thigh. The doctors said that my left leg was severely broken in at least eight places. The injuries had to be cleaned extensively, as the breaks were very dirty. I ran a high risk of infection. My family was told that I was missing ten inches of bone in my left femur, and two separate one-inch pieces of bone in my left tibia. Furthermore, they said that my leg did a complete 180-degree rotation during the crash, which had done an undetermined amount of damage to my knee. They did know, however, that the top of my left kneecap was partially shaved off, and my left hand was broken in at least five places. The doctors put plates in my left forearm just above and just below the wrist. They also had to remove my nail beds on my ring and middle fingers to set my broken fingertips. At the time of the crash, I was wearing acrylic nails—which were driven into my fingertips. Once they were set, my nail beds were sewn back on so that my nails would grow back properly.

Upon determining my condition, Dianna and Trish set up an on-line computer blog (majorlisa-taylor.blogspot.com) to keep everyone apprised of my condition. They updated it daily for the first couple of weeks. Later, once I was conscious and physically able, I updated it daily for a while, then weekly, and

External fixator

eventually monthly. People could write in and leave messages of hope and encouragement. This "window to the world" was and continues to be extremely therapeutic for me during my long and arduous recovery. We didn't immediately put a counter on the blog, but after 3 months, we placed a counter on it to see how much activity it was generating. Amazingly enough, at the time of this writing, the site has generated almost 55,000 hits! The number of people who were and continue checking on my progress humbles me.

Excerpt from the Blog

"Around 2:30 Friday afternoon Lisa Taylor and Mary Pfeifer were involved in a serious motorcycle accident in West Virginia. An impaired driver that went left of center hit them. Following the crash, Lt. Mary Pfeifer was treated and released from Wheeling Hospital on Friday with minor injuries. Major Lisa Taylor was transported from Wheeling Hospital on Friday, July 13 to the Trauma Center at Ruby Memorial/University Hospital in Morgantown, West Virginia. She is still critical but stable, and remains under heavy sedation. Last night's surgery successfully stabilized multiple broken bones in her

left leg and left wrist and arm. A subsequent surgery is scheduled for Sunday to further repair and irrigate her leg. There were no head or internal injuries, as both riders were wearing helmets. Lisa is receiving excellent care and doctors are keeping her comfortable, as she will undergo several more surgeries. Doctors were able to reconstruct her leg, and are very optimistic she will regain use of it. However, the surgeon described her leg as the worst break he had ever seen. Your continued thoughts and prayers are greatly appreciated; the family hopes to have her moved to a Columbus hospital around the middle of the week."

During my six-day stay at West Virginia University Hospital in Morgantown, the doctor's inserted a ten-inch piece of concrete in my left thigh to hold the place of my femur, and metal rods and screws were placed in my leg from hip to ankle. I regained partial consciousness on the second day at the hospital. I also had a wound vac on my leg to continuously extract the infection. I also received a total of seven blood transfusions during my stay at West Virginia University Hospital. I endured three surgeries while there. Throughout my stay, my dad, my sister, Trish, and other friends were with me.

In order to be closer to home, on my sixth day at West Virginia University Hospital, I was trans-ferred by ambulance to Grant Hospital, in Columbus, Ohio. My sister rode along with me, while my dad and Trish followed behind. There were two young men that drove the squad. The squad ride was both

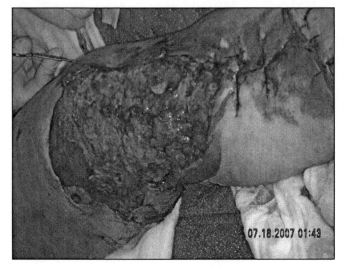

07.18.2007 01:43

My left leg after three surgeries

terrifying as well as excruciating. Not only did I feel

every bump, as they removed all intravenous pain

medication, but the driver drove at extreme speeds

as he struggled to stay awake. My sister fearfully

watched him in the rear view mirror as he fought

to keep his eyes open. We later found out that this

was the squad driver's second job. My sister pleaded

with the gentlemen to trade places to ensure our

safe arrival. The driver had to pull off into at least two rest areas to remain alert. His speeds were so high that dad and Trish could not legally keep up, so they called and said that they would just meet us at the hospital. Fortunately, we made it to Grant Hospital without being involved in another crash.

Excerpt from the Blog

"Lisa returned from surgery, and will be kept heavily sedated for a while so she can rest. The surgeon is still hopeful he can save her leg; he said, '"We haven't used all of our bag of tricks yet." He reminds us of Dr. House, if you've ever watched that TV show. He had a motorcycle crash 3 years ago and had to go through some intense surgery on his leg too. The doctor cleaned the wound again, and put

some more drains in her leg and arm. Several of your

messages tonight talked about Lisa's determination

and you could not be more right. She's got the right

attitude to overcome all odds, and she is prepared

for whatever God's will is for her. There is a young

man in a wheelchair named Donny who is about to

have his 20th surgery on his leg, he was involved in

a car crash in 2002 and has such a positive outlook

on life. His spirit is very similar to Lisa's. They

have talked briefly but plan to talk more when she

is feeling better. Keep both of them in your prayers.

Lisa is scheduled for another surgery on Monday,

providing the muscle flaps are good. Lisa was taken

into surgery around 5:30pm. The physical therapists

were here earlier this morning and had her stand up

on her good leg. It was extremely painful, but she

got through it. Between the physical therapist's exercise and the surgery today, she is going to feel like a train hit her - again. She appreciates all of you who have taken the time out of your busy lives to come and see her. Right now while she is undergoing multiple surgeries and would greatly appreciate it if you could come during the visitation hours or call the hospital first to ensure she is not in surgery, out for tests, or resting. She needs adequate time to recuperate between surgeries, visitors, and unexpected events. Also, she does not want for you to come here and then not get to see her."

I spent another twelve days in Grant's trauma unit. While there, the doctors continued to clean my wounds and perform muscle flap and skin grafts on my left leg. They had to take muscle from the back of my left calf, and wrap it around the front of my leg, as my leg had been totally degloved. Then, a large amount of skin graft was harvested from my upper right thigh in order to cover my left leg. Even though neither I, nor Mary experienced the typical "road rash" that bikers often do, I have to believe that skin grafting is just as painful. My plastic surgeon also repaired a shattered bone in my left hand between my wrist and little finger. I was told that the flesh on my leg had to heal before they could address the many orthopedic issues. I was given another two blood transfusions, as I had lost so much blood.

While the doctors were not initially optimistic that they could save my leg, they were even less optimistic that such a large area of skin grafts would adhere and actually grow. Miraculously, they were able to save my leg, and the entire skin graft, with the exception of a quarter-sized area on my knee adhered and grew. The huge skin graft covered three fourths of my left leg.

Like most women, I was not always satisfied with my appearance. I had often complained about how my legs were not in proportion with the rest of my body. My upper body was always quite small, while my legs were very thick and muscular. The doctors told me that had my calf muscles not been so large, they wouldn't have been able to wrap my calf muscles around to the front of my leg to replace the missing muscle. This would have necessitated taking large, painful muscle grafts from my back or other areas of my body. Again, God prepared me.

Trish continued to stay with me almost twenty-four hours a day, only going home to shower and change clothes. I will never forget her kindness, compassion, and generosity. She is the true definition of a person with a servant's heart.

Throughout my hospital stay, I was placed on a morphine drip, which caused me to itch constantly. To combat the itching, I was given Benadryl, which rendered me virtually unconscious. I was later placed on Percoset, which made me extremely ill, so finding the right drug combination was challenging at best.

I was totally non-weight bearing on my left leg, which was not problematic at that time, because moving in any fashion was excruciating. I was completely bedfast until my last week at Grant, when I asked the nurses if I could commandeer

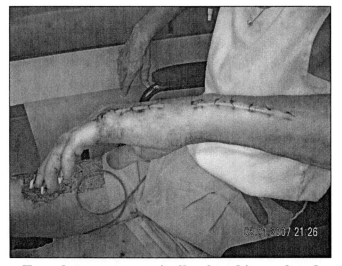

**Two plates were surgically placed in my hand
and forearm**

a wheelchair on two different occasions to take a
couple short strolls. Because I had been so accus-
tomed to being physically active, the inactivity was
almost unbearable. The hospital walls seemed to be
closing in on me. The staff procured a wheelchair
and my good friend, Elzie Fish—another biker friend
and former co-worker, took me for a walk around the

premises. On another occasion, my dad, sister, and Trish took me around the outside perimeter of the hospital. Those events were such victories in terms of my mental health. While every bump during the rides was terribly painful, the fact that I was moving was a step in the right direction.

A couple of days before my release, a social worker visited me and asked which nursing home I would prefer, as I could not adequately care for myself. I responded that I would like to stay in my home area, but that I did not have a preference. At that point, Trish spoke up and said that I would not be going to a nursing home that she would take care of me. I strongly objected and said that she could not accept that responsibility, nor would I let her. She argued sternly and eventually, I relented. Trish was on hiatus from

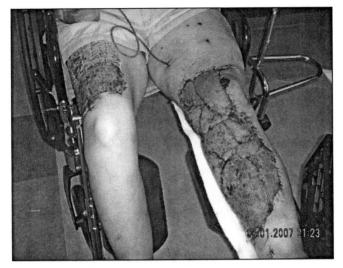

My leg after seven surgeries

work, as she was already caring for her mother, who had sustained a brain aneurysm three years earlier. My friendship with Trish, who ultimately became my main caregiver, had only begun a year or so before the crash. Without her assistance, I would have spent an extended period of time in a rehabilitation facility, because I simply could not care for myself.

<u>Excerpt from the Blog</u>

"Praise GOD I'm being released today after 18 days in the hospital! My first doctors' visit is Thursday. Hopefully being home with my dogs—Chrissy, Amy, and my cat, Sissy will do me worlds of good. Thanks again to my family and friends for helping me out in so many ways during this horrible ordeal. I keep thinking that this is a dream from which I will wake, but the reality is that I am in for months, if not years of therapy—but if GOD brings me to it, HE will bring me through it."

"People may fail many times, but they become failures only when they begin to blame someone else. Experience is determined by yourself — not the circumstances of your life"

-Gita Belli –

Chapter 6

True Friendship

"... The greatest love is shown when a person lays down his life for his friends..."(John 15:13)

Upon my arrival home, I discovered that my family already had a hospital bed delivered and set up in my living room, along with a whole host of other hospital equipment. I was on Lovenox for the prevention of blood clots, Percoset, Norco, Oxycontin, and Vicodin for the pain. For the never-ending nausea, I was prescribed Zofran and Phenergran. I also had to have a port inserted in my right arm to facilitate three weeks of intravenous antibiotics that I endured three times a day. I was told that I would be at risk of losing my leg for two to three years due to infection. If it were not for Trish keeping my medications straight, I would have been in real trouble. She not only doled out all the medications at just the right times, she often held my head when I became incapacitated from the nausea, and stayed up with me when I could not sleep–which was often. There was so much nerve damage to my left leg that it "buzzed" almost non-stop. In an effort to combat the constant discomfort, I was prescribed Lyrica. Through it all, Trish saw me at my absolute worst, yet still stayed to help me out. Many other friends graciously helped too. They cooked for me, mowed my grass, and handled other things that I had previously done and taken for granted. God had blessed me with wonderful friends!

"A candle loses nothing by lighting

another candle"

-Erin Majors-

At this point, God's plan started to become even more evident. About two years prior to the crash, my dad and I had built a wheelchair ramp for my mom to use, as she had been physically disabled from experiencing a brain aneurysm twenty years earlier. Unfortunately, she only had the opportunity to use it once before she died. I tried unsuccessfully to give the ramp away, simply to get it out of my garage. Who knew I would eventually need it?

Additionally, although my mom's disability mostly confined her to a wheelchair, she could walk short distances with a hemi (one-handed) walker. After my mom's passing, my sister, Terry kept her one-handed walker—which I eventually used. Who knew I'd need it?

Also, during that same time frame, I purchased a shower chair for my mom because she was preparing to visit. That too, after her passing, I tried unsuccessfully to give away. Who knew I would eventually need it as well?

And finally, I was anticipating foot surgery prior to the crash for an unrelated condition, and I had purchased a pair of crutches. While to date, I have never had the foot surgery, who knew I'd need the crutches after the crash?

After coming home from the hospital, I had a steady stream of well-wishers come to my house. Colonel Butch Collins—the new OSP superintendent, as well as the rest of my patrol family and friends were fantastic. I also received countless calls and cards, which really kept my spirits high. The Patrol assured me that I had one year of disability, so I was optimistic of returning to full duty after my recuperation.

After several weeks, I went to my plastic surgeon to see how the muscle flap and skin grafts had taken. The doctor was very pleased at how my leg had healed, although there was a half-dollar sized area on my knee where the graft did not take. His plan was to allow the knee to heal naturally before he would clear me for the orthopedic work. Until then, I was placed in hand therapy.

My orthopedic surgeon was also pleased with my progress. While he had only consulted with me thus far, he was very familiar with the orthopedic surgeons who had operated on me in Morgantown. He authorized non-weight bearing leg therapy and anxiously awaited the opportunity to complete the work that the West Virginia doctors had begun.

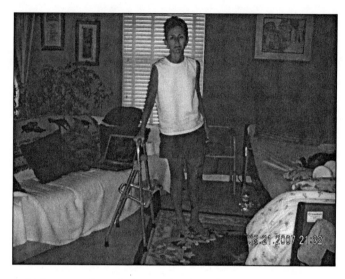

At home after being released from the hospital

Trish and me

Chapter 7

The Healing Process

"For His wounds have healed ours."

(1 Peter 2:24)

Although therapy was certainly necessary, it was *excruciating*. The therapists at Ohio Health, however, were excellent. They pushed me to increase the strength and dexterity of my left hand, as well as strengthen my left leg. We also worked to improve the flexibility of my badly damaged knee. For the following three months after my release from Grant Hospital, I pushed myself by working out two hours a day, and by first using my wheelchair to take my dogs for one mile walks, then later graduating to using my crutches for the routine excursions. I would use hand weights to strengthen my arms and do hundreds of crunches from my hospital bed to maintain my core strength. My pain was slowly decreasing daily, and my attitude and faith continued to gain momentum. I was feeling good, aside from the fact that I could not yet walk.

Excerpt from the Blog

"Yesterday's therapy session wasn't too bad. The therapy Nazi's simply wanted to measure my range of motion on my knee and ankle. They indicated that it was obvious that I'm working both joints on my

own and they were pleased. That encouraged me! My next session is next week."

After weeks of trying to allow my knee to heal naturally, my plastic surgeon decided to try another skin graft. I re-entered Grant Hospital for my eighth surgery. The doctor took a small two-inch by two-inch piece of skin from my upper left thigh to cover my knee. The orthopedic doctor would not operate until my flesh had completely healed due to fear of infection and rejection. While this was an attempt to speed the recovery so I could progress to the next surgery, the skin graft failed, forcing us to again attempt to allow the knee to heal naturally. Each week, I would visit my plastic surgeon, hoping that he would allow me to have the bone replaced in my leg. I anxiously awaited the surgery, as I knew that was the only way I would ever walk again.

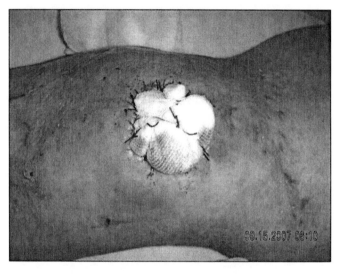

My second, and unsuccessful skin graft

In early October, my friends Dianna White, Ty and Don Grimwood, and a host of other friends, planned a benefit, auction, and motorcycle ride for Mary and me at Quaker Steak and Lube, in Columbus, Ohio.

Many people showed up to give donations and wish us well. As a result, money was raised via the motorcycle ride and auction in an effort to help us with our extensive and ever-increasing medical costs.

Rich "The Lube Guy," me and Mary at the benefit

In late October, representatives from the Patrol's human resource section paid me another visit. They indicated that although I had a year's worth of disability, if I did not return at the six-month mark, a Department of Public Safety committee would review my case. If it did not appear that I would return to work in the very near future, I would either be forced to take a disability retirement or the Division could separate me from service. I was assured that if I returned after six months, I could work in a "transitional" or "light duty" fashion for a year. This simply meant that I could return to work and perform administrative duties in civilian clothes, rather than in uniform. After the end of that year, hopefully, I would be able to pass my rigorous physical and weapons qualifications, ultimately proving that I would be fit for full duty. I was optimistic that my leg would be healed enough after a year of light duty that I could and would again wear a state trooper uniform.

Excerpt from the Blog

"While I was at the doctor's office, I met a young black lady—I didn't get her name, but I have to tell you how inspirational she was. She was 21 years old and about 2 years ago; she too was involved in a motorcycle crash. She indicated that an elderly lady turned left in front of her, causing her to crash her Suzuki 500 cc motorcycle. This resulted in both of her legs becoming severely damaged. Unfortunately, the doctors were unable to save her right leg, resulting in her becoming an amputee. Her amputation was just above her right knee. While she still walks with a

cane, she had such an unbelievably positive attitude.

She made me feel so optimistic!"

Finally, in early November, my plastic surgeon gave me the green light to see my orthopedic surgeon. After my visit, I was scheduled for surgery in mid-November. I was so excited about the upcoming surgery. I had no fear, as I knew that God had been with me throughout this ordeal. The doctor assured me that this operation would be easier than the previous ones and I could expect a two-day hospital stay.

Excerpt from the Blog

"My surgery is right around the corner and I can't wait! I know I'll be a bit sore, but I'm so excited to

walk again. My goal is to come back to work after the first of the year. Please pray that that occurs."

I was told that the surgeons would go into my right hip and bore down into my right femur to harvest a significant amount of bone and marrow to replace the missing bone in my left leg. They would combine my own bone with cadaver bone, collagen, and other compounds to create a "slush-like" material that would be placed into my left leg. Their hope was that it would eventually grow. During this surgery, my plastic surgeon would be there to open the flap he created, as not to interrupt any blood supply that was previously arranged. The plastic surgeon was also to take out the plate he put in my left hand between my wrist and little finger, as the bone had healed sufficiently, and the plate was impeding the use of my smallest finger.

Excerpt from the Blog

"Lisa went into surgery at 7:30am this morning and is now in recovery. The surgeon said everything went well and she will be in recovery for the next couple of hours. Her family and Trish are there with her. The surgeon was impressed with her positive attitude and said that can make such a difference on the final outcome. She will be kept at Grant Hospital for a couple days. Your continued prayers are appreciated, she is so anxious to return to work and a normal life."

I, however, was not prepared for the extreme pain I experienced after this surgery. What was supposed to be a two-day hospital stay, turned into five, because my right leg would not support me and I was severely anemic. Even the slightest movement caused tremendous pain. Thankfully, because I was in the orthopedic wing, my hospital bed had pulleys I could use to lift myself up. My blood count was extremely low and I was very lethargic. Even the slightest activity drained me, so I was given another two units of blood. I continued to be severely anemic, so my iron was greatly increased.

Excerpt from the Blog

"Well, here I sit at Grant Hospital on Sunday night. I was hoping I'd be released today, but had rough

night last night and a rough day today. My hemoglobin was low and I was running a little bit of a fever, so they decided to keep me. Where they harvested the bone from my right thigh as well as where they fixed 2 small grafts in my left calf were very sore. Unbelievably, where they fixed the 10-inch piece in my left thigh didn't hurt too incredibly bad. I did, however, feel like I'd been hit by a car..."

Before I was sent home, I was given a Simple Bledsoe leg brace, which allowed my knee to bend, yet provide the necessary support it needed.

It was not until two weeks after my release from the hospital, at a follow-up visit, I was told the reason for my tremendous pain. When I asked the doctor about why my pain was so intense, he indicated that while he and his surgical team were reaming my right leg for bone and marrow, they inadvertently poked a hole in my right femur—in essence breaking my leg, just above the knee. This caused significant pain. He stated that this was only the tenth procedure like this that he had ever performed and that they had to be very aggressive in harvesting as much bone as possible. The doctors placed more than 120 units of new bone in my left leg.

For two months following the orthopedic surgery, the simple act of standing on my good leg was excruciating. In fact, for two to three weeks after the surgery, I could not stand alone. My right knee swelled to two to three times its normal size and my left foot would became discolored and would swell significantly each day.

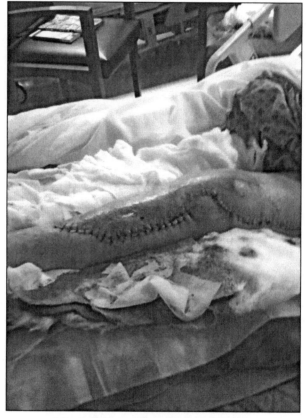

My left leg after nine surgeries

As I previously mentioned, one of my doctors who deals specifically with infections, told me that I would be at a great risk for infection for two to three years after the crash due to the amount of dirt, gravel, and debris I picked up from the roadway and the ditch line. Surprisingly—not once did I develop any type of infection after the crash, nor after any of the nine surgeries I underwent. God continued his protection.

Excerpt from the Blog

"On June 15th a friend and I rode our bicycles 70 miles to Zanesville and stopped a troop to talk to him about you. I had just gotten back into bicycling with a little bit of seriousness, as I was trying to get "back" into shape (feeling soft and fat), and I was looking for motivation. The overnight trip got me going, and I kept it up. Well, as your recovery started, I thought about doing some serious riding with a purpose – to reach 3000 miles from the 13th of June for the year. It was your recovery that motivated me, as I saw

no signs of self-pity, and a lot of gritty tough work and pain. I worked all summer at it and into the fall. Getting a full-time job put a crimp into my riding time. Winter brought a new challenge – COLD!!! Nevertheless, as my riding season was dedicated to your recovery effort, I decided I could not fall down on the job. I had a crank set meltdown yesterday afternoon and had to hitch a ride to the bike shop (with much dread). However, it was an easy fix, and I finished my 42-mile ride at 9PM. I have 2954 miles as of today since your accident. My lights and winter riding gear have gotten a workout (Even now as it is only 35 degrees, I am procrastinating by writing this e-mail!). I will ride the last 46 miles (since I started counting) this afternoon. You have shown a lot of courage. Your crutches have gotten a workout (don't fall any more). My 27-year-old Panasonic touring bike has too. Solidarity! Keep up the great work. I see a future of motivational speaking for you, and until you start talking, no one will know your story as you will get out of your chair and stroll briskly to the podium to begin – just like most everyone else. Gotta go ride." Note from Mike Hunter, retired OSP lieutenant

"Whatever course you decide upon,

there is always someone to tell you that you are

wrong. There are always difficulties arising, which

tempt you to believe that your critics are right.

To map out a course of action and follow it to

an end requires...courage"

-Ralph Waldo Emerson-

Chapter 8

The Great Disappointment

"If your faith were only the size of a mustard seed,

it would be large enough to uproot that mulberry

tree over there and send it hurtling into the sea."

(Luke 17:6)

In early January 2008, as I was anxiously making plans to return to work in February, I was again contacted by our human resources section and a bombshell was dropped. Although I was originally told that I could return to work in early February and work a year of transitional or light duty, I was informed that because I was an exempt officer (an officer holding the rank of lieutenant or above), I only had ninety days of available light duty. If my physician could not definitively indicate that I could return to full, unrestricted duty after three months, I would either be separated from the Patrol, or I would be forced to retire. If I were to be separated, I would only have two years of return to work rights should I recover sufficiently to return to my previous position. Furthermore, after my maximum one-year disability benefits ran out, I would receive no pay–so that was not a viable option for me. If I chose to take a disability retirement, I would be entitled to five years return to work rights and at least receive approximately sixty-two percent of my salary. So, with a heavy heart, I contacted the retirement board and started the disability retirement process. I had spent well over half of my life with the Ohio State Highway Patrol and had such a passion for public safety, so I was devastated.

I began the arduous process of collecting the medical documentation necessary for the retirement board to approve my disability. I had to obtain records from Wheeling, West Virginia University, and Grant Hospitals, as well as information from my plastic and orthopedic surgeons. Once my orthopedic surgeon, indicated that I was totally and permanently disabled from my position as trooper, the retirement board would have me meet with it's independent physician to determine whether or not he or she would concur with the previous doctor's findings.

<u>Excerpt from the Blog</u>

"I write this with a heavy heart because I now know that I must file for disability retirement very soon. I had planned to return to light duty on February 4th, 2008, but will be unable to do so because my doctor cannot definitively say that I will be prepared to return to full duty in 90 days. I have great love and passion for my job, as I have given almost 25 years of my life to the OSP. It disheartens me that I will be leaving this great organization and its great people this way. One good thing is that I have 5 years "come back" rights. So, if I can progress and heal, my hearts desire is to return to full duty as soon as possible. With God's grace and mercy, I hope to make that happen. Please continue to pray for healing, as I really would love to finish my career the way I intended. One thing I

do know is that God is in control and that everything will be okay. He doesn't close one door unless He opens another. My finite mind doesn't understand why things happened this way, but I have to believe that there's a lesson or a purpose here. I just need to be sensitive to His plans. In the meantime, I plan to work very hard at rehab and finish my MBA."

On January 28, 2008, I again visited my orthopedic surgeon to determine if the bone grafts had healed sufficiently to start bearing weight on my left leg. January, as it seemed, was not going to be a good month. The doctor told me that while the grafts were healing nicely, he was not satisfied that they would yet support me. He continued my non-weight bearing status for another two months. Again, I was crushed. I left the doctor's office in tears.

In mid March, I visited the retirement board's doctor at the Orthopedic Center for Excellence in Columbus, Ohio. I had collected CAT scans, MRIs, as well as x-rays as instructed in preparation for my visit. As the doctor walked through the door, he said, "Lisa, after reading your orthopedic doctor's notes, I really did not need to see you." He indicated that he could discern from the notes that I was permanently and totally disabled from law enforcement. When I asked him if I would ever be a trooper again, he replied, "not likely." I told him that it would be my mission to prove him wrong. His advice to me was, "find a job that is about fifty-percent sedentary." My response was, "that's not going to happen."

After hearing the finality of the doctor's opinion, I knew that I had to go and clean out my office so that whomever would be taking my place as commander could move in. I hadn't set foot inside the Shipley Building since my crash. It simply had been too emotional for me. So, I went in to pack up my personal belongings on a Sunday—so I wouldn't have to see anyone. Even though it was heart wrenching and tearful, it was good to have closure. I would eventually return to visit my friends at the Shipley Building—but this wasn't the day.

During my 25-year career with the Ohio State Highway Patrol, I had built a considerable bank of sick time. Consequently, I had 800-900 hours of sick leave available to supplement my income. This income ensured that I continued to get paid at almost my full rate while awaiting my approval for disability retirement. Furthermore, I had always tried to be wise in my investments and saved for a "rainy day." That day had finally come. Because I had always attempted to live frugally and well within my means, I was not financially devastated. While I lost a considerable amount of my income by being forced to take a disability retirement, my previous planning had paid off. Because of that, as well as my great insurance, not one bill went unpaid. This nest egg proved to be invaluable in my early retirement. More importantly, I was never unable to pay my church tithe. God continued to work his miracles.

"We need to understand that thoughts are tools.

Are we using them as productively as we can?

Are our thoughts serving us well,

or are we their victims?

It's up to us."

-Dr. Tom Morris-

Chapter 9

The Trial

"Yes, each of us will give an account of himself

to God." (Romans 14:12)

I n early February, Mary and I attended the third pretrial of our case. Because of our injuries, we were unable to attend the first two. My good friend, Captain Tina Phillips, of the West Virginia State Police attended the first two in our absence. She graciously provided us updates regarding the pending trial. Upon our arrival, Mary and I walked into the magistrate's court lobby, right past Mr. Walenciej. There had been such a transformation in his appearance that we did not recognize him. He had showered, shaved, and was in a business suit. We did not realize that we had walked by him until we reached the jury room, where one of the deputies who had assisted with the investigation told us. We then discussed how different he looked today versus his disheveled appearance at the crash scene.

It was during this pretrial that we discovered that Mr. Walenciej's attorney was filing a motion to suppress the blood test. In addition to John admitting to Oxycontin and a litany of antidepressants, the toxicology report revealed that he also had Valium in his system as well as cocaine metabolites. At my worst physical condition, I was only taking forty milligrams of Oxycontin. Amazingly enough, Mr. Walenciej,

Mr. John Walenciej preparing for court

admittedly, was driving while taking eighty milli-

grams of the same drug. While the drug served

its purpose well during my recovery, it was Mr.

Walenciej's addiction that drove me to end my

dependence on that narcotic. I saw firsthand the effects of addiction to prescription narcotics.

We were told that the motion to suppress hearing would be scheduled for late February. Mary and I made plans to attend. It was also during this time that Mary discovered that she would have to have surgery also in February due to the herniated disc in her neck.

In late February, I attended the motion to suppress hearing. Mr. Walenciej's attorney argued that in his opinion, the blood test was not taken legally; there- fore, it should be suppressed. After testimony from one of the investigating officers from the Ohio County Sheriff's Office, as well as arguments from the prosecutor, the magistrate ruled in our favor. She indicated that the test would remain. The defense attorney, however, felt that the magistrate over-stepped her bounds, so he promised to file a writ to appeal her decision. The next pre-trial was scheduled for April 10, 2008.

Also during that visit, I finally visited the trucking terminal where our crash occurred. It took a long time for me to gather the courage to visit the scene and to thank those individuals from the trucking company who so selfishly assisted Mary and me. The trucking company employees were shocked that the doctors had been able to save my leg and they were pleased that Mary and I were both on the mend.

The return of some semblance of normalcy to my life was on March 31, 2008. This is when my orthopedic doctor finally gave me permission to start bearing weight on my left leg. He said to take it slow, as walking would not occur overnight. He declined to place me in formal rehabilitation at that time, as he wanted me to simply become acclimated to weight bearing, walking, and rolling my foot. I was instructed to practice putting a little more weight on my left leg each day until I did not need my crutches. Once he placed me in rehabilitation, he said, the "hard work would begin." I would eventually be doing knee bends and lunges, as well as other necessary, but excruciatingly painful exercises. That did not frighten me, however, I was extremely excited about starting to walk again. It had been eight and a half months!

As I stated earlier, I had been in the middle of my MBA program at Franklin University when I was hit. While I wasn't happy about the interruption of my degree, it actually gave me a purpose as I recovered. On April 1, 2008, I resumed working on my master's degree. Working on my education filled the endless hours that I was either confined to a bed or wheelchair.

"The place to improve the world is first in one's own heart, head and hands"

-Robert M. Pirsig-

On April 10, 2008, we attended yet another pretrial. During the hearing, we discovered that when the lab was conducting its tests on Mr. Walenciej, the lab personnel, unfortunately, ran out of blood sample. While cocaine metabolites were present, the amount of cocaine could not be quantified. So, rather than prejudice the jury with the cocaine information, it was simply thrown out. While the blood test would remain, the mention of cocaine would be redacted. The next pretrial date was scheduled for May 30, 2008.

On Wednesday, May 27, 2008, I received a call from John Little, the prosecuting attorney in Wheeling, West Virginia. He informed me that he had just received a call that Mr. Walenciej had committed suicide earlier in the week. He did not know all the details, but it was his understanding that Mr. Walenciej had shot himself.

<u>Newspaper Article (May 30, 2008)</u>

WALENCIEJ, John Paul, 43, of Brilliant, Ohio,

passed away.

There will be no visitation or service at this time.

A Memorial service for John will be announced at a

later date.

Of course, I was devastated. It is my belief that there is nothing worth taking your own life over. I immediately contacted my family and Mary, as well as the litany of people who have assisted with the case. Mary and I requested prayer for the Walenciej family, as they had lost a son and a brother. The criminal case, of course, was dismissed.

A day or so after the tragic phone call, I sat down and wrote Mr. Walenciej's significant other the following note:

Dear Michael,

I am the driver of the motorcycle that John hit last year. I wanted to express my sincere sympathy for your loss. I cannot imagine how you feel right now.

Even though John changed my life forever, please know that I forgave him long ago. And even though I wanted closure and wanted to move on with my life, I certainly never wanted it in this manner. I believe there is nothing worth taking ones life over.

I pray that with time you and your family heal from this tragedy and seek comfort from above.

May God bless you

Mary and I both felt that John should serve some type of jail sentence—not only for punishment for his crime, but to help remove his dependence on prescription drugs. Unfortunately, I never heard back from the family.

Two Wolves

(Author Unknown)

One evening an old Cherokee told his grandson about a battle that goes on inside people. He said, "My son, the battle is between two "wolves" inside us all. One is evil. It is anger, envy, jealousy, sorrow, regret, greed, arrogance, self-pity, guilt, resentment, inferiority, lies, false pride, superiority, and ego.

The other is good. It is joy, peace, love, hope,

serenity, humility, kindness, benevolence, empathy,

generosity, truth, compassion and faith." The

grandson thought about it for a minute and then

asked his grandfather: "Which wolf wins?" The old

Cherokee simply replied, "The one you feed."

Chapter 10

My Life Resumed

"What is faith? It is the confident assurance that

something we want is going to happen. It is the

certainty that what we hope for is waiting for us,

even though we cannot see it up ahead."

(Hebrews 11:1)

My retirement from the division was effective April 27, 2008, and my executive officer, Captain David Dicken and his wife Fran hosted a very nice open house at their home to celebrate my retirement. Several OSP senior staff members, my family, as well as many of my co-workers attended. I originally told David that I did not want to have any sort of retirement party, as exiting the Patrol this way was so emotional for me. Dave and Fran assured me that it would be low-key and that I would not have to speak. They made the event very comfortable and memorable. I can never thank them enough for their kindness.

Excerpt from the Blog

"Well, my retirement is official. Thanks to Dave and Fran Dicken for opening their home for the wonderful send-off! Also thanks to everyone for such kind words, cards, and gifts. I have been so blessed with wonderful friends. You guys and gals have been nothing but stellar during this ordeal. The rehab

continues with my leg. I continue to walk 1-3 miles a day either with crutches or cane, but I am working to put more weight on it each day. I return to the doctor the middle of this month to determine if I can be placed in formal rehab. For now, I'm just trying to become acclimated to walking again."

As it turned out, I needed twenty-five years with the Patrol to secure an adequate pension. At the time of my retirement, I had served 25.1 years with the Ohio State Highway Patrol. Another God thing!

Also, interestingly enough, back in 2005, I had purchased a Harley-Davidson Road King trike (3-wheeled motorcycle) for my dad, as he was entering his early seventies. His riding abilities were still impeccable, however, I was beginning to worry about his ability to hold up the weight of a traditional motorcycle. The purchase was to simply give me more peace of mind. Who knew that I would be the one riding it in 2008?

In late April, my dad brought his trike to my home and left it for me to ride. He had promised to do that once I could walk. He had taken a lot of grief from the rest of our family for encouraging me to ride again. Only he and I understood the passion that we both share for motorcycling. In the first two weeks of having the trike, I rode well over three hundred miles. I was able to modify the way I shifted to accommodate my disability. Dad took my Harley Davidson Softail Deluxe home so he would have something to ride. Riding was as easy and refreshing as breathing.

It was so good to be back on a bike! During 2008, I rode over 15,000 miles.

In late May 2008, I was given permission from my orthopedic doctor to resume therapy. When I stopped therapy in November, just prior to the bone grafting, I could only bend my left knew approximately 49 degrees. Surprisingly, when I returned to therapy in May, my knee bent an amazing 70 degrees! God was continuing to show his power. Therapy was extremely painful, but I could see improvements almost daily. For months (even before becoming weight-bearing), I had been walking one to three miles a day on crutches to build my endurance and stamina. This painful, yet necessary endeavor had paid off in huge dividends!

On June 26th, I completed my first 5K walk at the Pickerington, Ohio Violet Festival. I was the only person walking with two canes and I came in dead last—but I finished! I jokingly told everyone that I came in first in the handicapped division. In September, I finished my second 5K race—again with two canes—in the Night Moves event in German Village, Columbus, Ohio. Slowly, but surely, my speed, mobility, and footing were improving.

In July, the motorcycle club I belong to hosted a motorcycle ride throughout southern Ohio. My dad, my brother, and my nephew rode their motorcycles up to Columbus to participate. During the ride, my dad complained of pain in his left side. We discussed him making a doctor's appointment for the next week. Dad was convinced that it was a kidney stone,

My first 5K after the crash

as he had experienced those many times. During his

doctor's visit, a CAT scan was performed. He did, in

fact, have kidney stones in his left kidney, but unfortunately the scan also revealed a baseball size mass attached to his duodenum on his right side. A preliminary biopsy indicated that it was not cancer. The doctors felt that it was some sort of ulcer—but that it had to be removed, as it was in a very critical area.

On July 28, my dad underwent surgery. When the doctors performed the procedure, they determined that the mass was, in fact, cancer, and it had grown to the size of softball. Dad had to have a Whipple procedure where the doctors removed half of his stomach, half of his pancreas, part of his bile duct, and a portion of his small intestine. The mortality rate for this particular surgery was very high. Fortunately, his physician said the surgery was a success and that he believed he was able to get all the cancer. But, five days after the surgery, dad was allowed to start taking small amounts of liquid by mouth. To our horror, shortly after he had ingested some liquid, he started experiencing excruciating pain and had to be taken back into emergency surgery. The incisions from the first Whipple procedure had failed, causing the liquid and bile from his stomach to be released into his abdominal cavity. Dad immediately became septic and nearly died. He spent the next two months in the hospital and a nursing facility when he underwent rehabilitation.

Due to my crash and early retirement, I was able to spend nearly every night in the hospital with my dad after his extensive surgery. The time I spent with him was some of the most precious I could remember. We had always been close, but I know that his near-death experience brought us even closer. I will always cherish that time.

In mid summer, my good friend and former colleague, Steve Belyus approached Trish and me about a potential business venture. Steve was a retired sergeant from the Patrol who had his own traffic crash reconstruction-consulting firm. Steve and I had previously worked together in southern Ohio. He knew that I was preparing to complete my degree and wanted to capitalize on my education in the business arena. While he is a gifted traffic crash reconstructionist, he recognized that he did not have the time or the skill sets needed to make his business flourish. He proposed that he conduct the actual traffic crash reconstructions, while Trish, who has an accounting degree and experience in network administration; handle the business office end of the endeavor. I was asked to handle the marketing and public relations component of the business. So, we collectively developed a business plan, established our vision, mission, goals, core values, and logo design, and formed Stars Consulting (Scientific Traffic Accident Reconstruction Specialists)—a limited liability company.

On September 23, 2008, I finished my master's degree from Franklin University. Because finishing my degree was such a milestone in this journey, I also asked my orthopedic surgeon if I could also finish formal therapy the same day, as I was faithfully doing therapy at home. I was walking two to three miles a day—and had recently added the elliptical to my training regimen. While I still used a cane most of the time, I was now able to walk short distances with no assistance. My doctor agreed that I had made extraordinary progress thus far, and he believed that I would continue to push myself and heal. When September 23 came, I was ecstatic! Two major hurdles had been overcome and it was time to celebrate.

Trish, dad, Terry, and me at graduation

The week after school and therapy ended, Trish and I left on a celebratory motorcycle trip. In twelve days, we traveled through ten states, and rode over 3,500 miles on the trike. The trip was both liberating and exhilarating! We traveled through Ohio, Kentucky, Tennessee, North Carolina, Georgia, South Carolina, Virginia, Maryland, Delaware, and finally—West Virginia. During our travels we also rode the length of the Outer Banks, which was one of the highlights of our trip. We ended the trip in West Virginia by design—I had come full-circle. I wanted a fresh start where this journey began.

Because of my employment with the Patrol and personal conviction, I have always had a passion for removing drunk/impaired drivers from our highways. So, on November 6, 2008, I visited the Ohio office of MADD (Mothers Against Drunk Driving). I met with the executive director and his staff to discuss potential volunteering opportunities. While I had worked with MADD on numerous safety events as a state trooper, I felt that I could offer them something that was unique—the ability to speak about impaired driving from the perspectives of both a law enforcement officer who has taken hundreds of impaired drivers from the highways—and from that of a victim.

While I was not exactly sure where my expertise would be most beneficial for this worthwhile organization, we discussed various opportunities it offered—the VIP (Victim Impact Panel), advocacy, and potential testimonials at legislative sessions. I do believe that people need to understand that there is a significant cost to impaired driving—physical, financial, and emotional. If I can reach just one person, then my efforts will not have been in vain.

In November, I applied for and was accepted as an adjunct professor at Ohio University. In late 2008, I began teaching in the area of law enforcement and hoped to soon teach business classes as well.

"It is not falling into the water, but lying in it,

that drowns"

-Anonymous-

Early in my career, while I was a trooper working out of the Bucyrus, Ohio patrol post, I stopped a 16-year old young man for speeding. His name was Scott Rike. Unbeknownst to me, he later developed a keen interest in the OSP and later became an Ohio state trooper. Little did we know how our lives would become so similar? Just before my crash, Scott, who only had only been on the Patrol for about six years, developed a life-threatening disease that temporarily ended his career. He was devastated by his physical condition and by the fact that he had to leave the career he so loved. Also during that time, he and his wife, Tammy lost their first child during her pregnancy. He was at one of the lowest points in his life. After my crash, we became close friends, corresponding by email, phone, and by letters. We became support for one another during our recoveries and our career losses. Also during this time, both of our fathers developed very similar cancers. Unfortunately, Scott's dad's cancer was diagnosed late and he soon succumbed to the disease. Without God's hand in our lives, Scott and I would have never met, become friends, and lived what I believe to be parallel lives. Fortunately, Scott is now in remission and back to work with the Patrol. Additionally, he and his wife succeeded in their attempt to have a baby. They now have a beautiful son—and another on the way! Scott was such an inspiration and source of strength for me during my recovery. His faith was contagious and helped further strengthen my relationship with God.

I received this verse and story from a friend by email. While I don't know the author, when I read it, I was a gentle reminder that God is continuing to refine me.

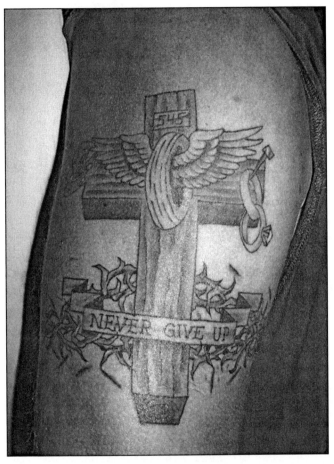

Sergeant Scott Rike's tattoo

"Like a refiner of silver, He will sit and closely watch as the dross is burned away. He will purify the Levites, the ministers of God, refining them like gold or silver, so that they will do their work for God with pure hearts." (Malachi 3:3)

This verse puzzled some women in a Bible study and they wondered what this statement meant about the character and nature of God. One of the women offered to find out the process of refining silver and get back to the group at their next Bible Study. That week, the woman called a silversmith and made an appointment to watch him at work. She didn't mention anything about the reason for her interest beyond her curiosity about the process of refining silver. As she watched the silversmith, he held a piece of silver over the fire and let it heat up. He explained that in refining silver, one needed to hold the silver in the middle of the fire where the flames were hottest as to burn away all the impurities. The woman thought about God holding us in such a hot spot; then she thought again about the verse that says: "He sits as a refiner and purifier of silver." She asked the silversmith if it was true that he had to sit there in front of the fire the whole time the silver was being refined. The man answered that yes, he not only had to sit there holding the silver, but he had to keep his eyes on the silver the entire time it was in the fire. If the silver was left a moment too long in the flames, it would be destroyed. The woman was silent for a moment. Then she asked the silversmith, "How do you know when the silver is fully refined?" He smiled at her and answered, "Oh, that's easy — when I see my image in it."

Chapter 11

Giving Thanks in Adversity

"For just as the heavens are higher than the earth, so are My ways higher than yours, and My thoughts than yours." (Isaiah 55:9)

Over the last two years, I have told count-less people that more good things have happened as a result of my crash, than bad. That is a statement that is probably very difficult to understand unless you have walked in my shoes. Aside from the physical and emotional trauma, because I was forced to take an early disability retirement, I was significantly impacted financially.

I think that in some ways, my crash couldn't have happened at a better time. By God's grace, I had just enough time to retire. I cringe to think what would have happened to me had the crash occurred when I only had five or ten years on the Patrol. It also forced me to slow down and appreciate life much more than I had ever done. In other ways, the crash couldn't have happened at a worse time. The Patrol was and continues going through some extremely tumultuous times due to leadership changes and internal conflict. I would like to think that I might have been able to help "fight the fight," but we'll never know.

While I certainly wish that the crash had not occurred, I have grown tremendously from it.

Through my injuries, surgeries, and rehabilitation, my faith in God became stronger; I have an even better relationship with my family. The outpouring of thoughts, prayers, and concern from my friends was truly humbling. I have realized that forgiveness is more healing for ourselves than for the ones we are forgiving. I also learned that the road to rehabilitation is difficult—but rewarding. I had to work so hard to take that first step—but what a glorious moment that was! I have had opportunities as a result of this incident that I would have never had. I have developed contacts and associations with people that I would never before would have. This incident has given me a lot of time to write, reflect, and volunteer for worthwhile causes. I have always enjoyed working with people and this journey has allowed me to tell my story and educate others about the perils of impaired driving. I have had the opportunity to speak with drivers' education classes, civic organizations, and volunteer with Mothers Against Drunk Driving (MADD). But, most importantly, God has given me great insight. I may not be able to control my circumstances, but I can control how I react to them. We can expect adversities and find opportunities and learn from them. That is just what I intend to do. I know bad things happen to good people, but in those bad things, we can grow and stretch ourselves beyond our wildest imaginations.

I was probably the most impatient person I knew. Through this journey, I have learned patience. I wanted things to happen in *my* time—but they didn't. Everything happens in *God's* time. Over the past couple of years, after enduring nine surgeries that included muscle, skin, and bone grafts, I had to learn considerable patience in learning to walk again. I did not use my left leg for eleven months. Even then, it was months before my leg would totally support me in taking the first step. So, although I will probably always have a noticeable limp, if that is the only physical remnant of this ordeal—I considered myself extremely blessed. It is also a daily reminder that *His grace is sufficient*—no matter my circumstances.

My good friend and former colleague, Scott Borden often used a saying that has since become my mantra—"the only things we control in life are our attitudes and efforts." I may be physically disabled, but I absolutely refuse to allow that to define me. My hope is that God will use me to bring good from this situation — that I may help others through tragedy — as He, my family, and many friends have helped me.

While it is unclear now whether I will ever return to the OSP, I do know that whatever happens will be for the best. God has been grooming me for ever-increasing challenges throughout my life. And now, I must be patient and listen for His calling. I will willingly go wherever He takes me.

I would like to close with a prayer I recently heard in church. I found it to be extremely fitting for not only my situation, but for that of our country in these spiritually, economically, and politically tumultuous times.

The Prayer of Sir Francis Drake

"Disturb us, Lord, when we are too well pleased

with ourselves,

When our dreams have come true because

we have dreamed too little,

When we arrived safely because we sailed

too close to the shore.

Disturb us, Lord, when with the abundance

of things we possess

We have lost our thirst for the waters of life;

Having fallen in love with life, we have ceased

to dream of eternity

And in our efforts to build a new earth,

we have allowed our vision of the new

Heaven to dim.

Disturb us, Lord, to dare more boldly,

to venture on wider seas

Where storms will show your mastery;

Where losing sight of land, we shall find the stars.

We ask You to push back the horizons of our hopes;

And to push into the future in strength, courage,

hope, and love."

"A happy person is not a person in a certain

set of circumstances, but rather a person with

a certain set of attitudes"

-Hugh Downs-

CPSIA information can be obtained
at www.ICGtesting.com
Printed in the USA
FFOW05n0349060417